NAPPY-HEADED
NEGRO SYNDROME

By ONEITA JACKSON

DAKOTA AVENUE WEST PUBLISHING

Detroit, Michigan

www.dakotavenuewest.com

Praise for
Nappy-Headed Negro Syndrome

*"Jack Kerouac called it the 'naked lunch, a frozen
moment when everyone sees what is on the end
of every fork.' These moments of revelation are
afforded by the greatest works of literature—Zen
teaching stories, Sufi tales about Nasruddin,
Aesop's Fables. Everyday life is delusional because
human beings are heavily defended from reality:
When there is a murder next door, they say,
'This never happens in our neighborhood,' and
then there is the notion 'I can do no wrong' that
results in the delirious cases of road rage that are
so puzzling and pervasive. In Oneita Jackson's*
Nappy-Headed Negro Syndrome, *we come
face-to-face with the deepest taboos in the
American psyche. Jackson, with humor and
compassion, shows us the quality of the paradoxes
that make us who we are—that make us so
stubborn, dangerous, and unrepentant."*

– JON WOODSON,
"Endowed: A Comic Novel"

"These are poetry of a high order. With an extraordinarily consistent tone, these are simultaneously transcendent and earthy. Every-day profoundly provocative. I think everyone should read them. (And it's wonderful to see pieces that give the reader credit for thinking.)"

– ALEX CRUDEN, editor

Nappy-Headed Negro Syndrome
is dedicated to

*"the people at formal events who assumed
we were The Help."*

First Lady Michelle Obama
Tuskegee University, 2015

I have lived in five U.S. cities, worked at 30-something jobs, hung out with people from all over the world. There are people who have always encouraged me and my pen or are interested in what I have to say. There are people who believe in my writing and love, appreciate, accept, and support me unconditionally. I would run out of ink naming you all.

THANK YOU.

Contents

Learning a Wing or Two

They don't take the EBT card at Neiman Marcus or Saks Fifth Avenue.

They don't take it at the Detroit Athletic Club or the Detroit Yacht Club.

They don't take the EBT card at Coach Insignia or The Whitney, and they damned sure don't take it at the Captain Jay's on Six Mile and Gratiot.

This I learned from a manager in the Captain Jay's parking lot.

My friend Paulette and I were hanging out; I left the driving to her. We'd just come from the Popeye's across the street—red beans and rice, two drumsticks. I'm not often in the vicinity of a Captain Jay's, known in the streets for its crack chicken, so when I see one, I start fiending.

And I needed some Captain Jay's—two chicken wings.

That was what prompted our impromptu information session on the chicken-wing payment policy: I asked the woman how much was one wing.

Chris Rock.

Isaac Hayes.

I'ma gitchoo.

"What method of payment are you using?" she asked, kindly.

She was standing a few feet from the car. I had called out to her because the Captain Jay's digital billboard was broken.

"What method of payment am I using?" I mouthed to myself. This was an odd question, considering we were not in a department store.

"Yes, because we don't take the EBT card."

They don't take the EBT card I don't have at the chicken-wing joint. (Poor woman, she was trying to save me from embarrassment.)

"They take it at the other Captain Jay's, but we don't take it here."

I smiled brightly—too brightly—nodded, and whispered.

"We have cash."

"You have an EBT?" she asked, misreading my glee.

"We have cash," I said a little louder, but not loudly enough.

I wanted her to come closer.

She did.

"We have money."

"Oh, OK."

"Now, how much is a chicken wing?"

She told me the price of the wings—three for $2.69, plus one dollar for frying—and offered, sweetly, "I'll take your order."

I placed my order for three wings and we proceeded to the drive-thru, where I paid with 14 quarters, one dime, one nickel, four pennies.

The Motherfucker with the Shoes

The question was merely of onomastics,
yet the Prescient One deigned to answer,
communicating to me in so so certain terms that
I was not now in a position to ask about, nor
had I been invited to make observations of, such
esoteric matter.

It was his shoes.
Very nice shoes.
What kind were they?

100% Certified Callipygian. Stamp here.

"Very expensive."

Very expensive shoes
Shoes so expensive,
have no name.

Name drop.

Gucci, Ferragamo, Yves St. Laurent
Shoes so expensive,
my mirrored closet.

"Oh, then you can afford these."

We. Have. Arrived.

Detroit cab driver with Washington, D.C., big shot.

Shoe name get.

I forgot.

Airport, please.

Job Search for Tomorrow

I haven't had to look for a job in 14 years, so I'm a little rusty on the process this millennium, but apparently it goes something like this: show up to a business unannounced, wear your sweatpants, take your six-foot-four German friend Yannick with you, ask for the person who does the hiring, and say you're on a first-name basis with her.

I was hipped to this new process when I went to Neiman Marcus looking for my friend Muffy.

My friend Muffy is the visual director at Neiman Marcus, Somerset, and she looks like a Muffy. When you say her name you have to say it like Thurston Howell III: "Muf-faaay." Muffy works all over the store and when I'm in there, I stop to say hello.

On this day I didn't see her, so I asked an associate to call her.

"Is Muffy here?"

"I'm not sure."

As the woman dialed, another Neiman Marcus associate waved to me from the escalator.

"That's my friend's mom," I said.

"Who, Renee?" the associate asked, cradling the phone.

"Yes."

"Are you applying for a job?"

"No, Muffy is my friend."

"Who, Renee?"

Renee is a black woman, a sophisticated black woman. An elegant woman.

Muffy's not there.

"Would you like to leave a message?"

"No, Muffy is my friend. I live across the street from her."

"Oh, she's your *friend*?"

The Syndrome.

Carded

Many years ago, the Neiman Marcus on Wisconsin Avenue in Washington, D.C., found a Howard University student buying a small item, a hat. The store didn't take my credit card and I didn't have enough cash. When I asked the associate what other methods of payment the store accepted, she asked if I had a Neiman Marcus card. I didn't. "That's it?" I asked. "Well," she offered reluctantly, "we take the Bergdorf Goodman card."

There is only one Bergdorf Goodman in the world. It is a New York City institution for insanely rich people who can afford insanely high prices for insanely nice clothes.

I didn't know Bergdorf Goodman owned Neiman Marcus, but I handed her my Bergdorf card, which they don't take at the Captain Jay's on Six Mile and Gratiot in Detroit.

Driving Miss Oneita

The doorman doesn't move.

The valet doesn't move.

I doesn't move.

They is impotent.

I is important.

I is in my yellow cab waiting for some service at the Detroit Athletic Club.

"What are you doing?" the doorman mouths from his place.

I is deaf.

I is dumb.

I is defiant.

"What are you doing?" he asks, now at my window, when I doesn't move from my place.

"I'm having lunch is what I'm doing."

And I is waiting for him to open my door so I can make my entrance.

Doorman moves.

Valet moves.

I move.

"Thank you."

High-heeled black boots; fleur-de-lis tights; black dress; grandmother's vintage coat, Fordham Road, the Bronx; black shades.

I is fly.

My friend is a Grosse Pointe woman who belongs to the DAC; she and I are in a group that meets there. She was the first woman to integrate the group and had to fight to get in.

I didn't.

The man who runs it invited me.

(My friend loves when I tell this story.)

Audio Visual

They don't get out much in Southfield, or much doesn't get out to them, it seems, because when I arrive at the movie theater, I am greeted by a Nappy-Headed Ticket Agent who takes one look at my Nappy-Headed ass and decides she will be starring in the role of Unsolicited Movie Reviewer.

Engagement with me beyond "enjoy the show," however, is simply unnecessary.

Roll tape.

Roll sound.

"Two tickets to 'Queen,' please," I say and turn to my Nappy-Headed friend. (We dropped off my Curly-Headed and Straight-Haired Indian friends at the door.)

"That's a Indian movie!"

The movie I want to see is not the movie I want to see.

I stare at Little Miss Nappy and repeat sternly:

"Two. Tickets. To. 'Queen.' Please."

(For Blaxploitation flicks, we have Bounce TV, King's Dream, free, at last, thank God, almighty.)

Next time, I will not miss my cue to state the obvious.

"'Bollywood Movie Reviewer' starring Oneita Jackson as Miss Too Much, Take Two":

Roll tape.

Roll sound.

"Two tickets to 'Queen,' please."

"That's a Indian movie!"

"YOU'RE A TICKET AGENT!"

Guest Who?

The Scene
Anna Wintour would have been pleased.

I certainly was. I looked like I stepped off the cover of Vogue magazine and was staring at myself a little too long.

This self-adulation was interrupted by a woman who had spilled something on her dress. She looked like she belonged on the cover of a Walmart circular and should have taken more care.

We were in the powder room at a little club in Grosse Pointe. It was so exclusive that the only people who looked like me were wearing black-and-white service attire and were parking cars, serving food, and clearing tables.

I helped the woman in distress get herself together and that is when things became interesting.

Event
Annual black-tie dinner for a private Detroit

club.

Access
I am the date of a gentleman from Chicago.

Me
Dupioni silk gown, chocolate A-line, velvet tessellated overlay.

Silk halter, chocolate cowl neck with ruching at back zipper.

Stuart Weitzman cowboy boots, chocolate-leather front, black pony-hair back, chocolate-leather lacing at calf.

Chocolate Bottega Venetta intreccio sunglass case, handbag.

Short, chic haircut.

Her
Rayon-polyamide tank top, black.

Nondescript ankle-length skirt, black.

Square, low-heel pumps, black.

Blunt blond bob.

Transaction

"We've been waiting for you."

Furrowed brow. I don't know this woman. Wait, I'm Oneita Jackson. My reputation precedes me. But wait, I don't know this woman.

"You've been waiting for *me*?"

Wait, she must know my date. He's from Chicago and his reputation precedes him, but I don't know this white woman.

"Yes, we've been waiting for you."

You can't be waiting for me 'cause I 'on' even know you, lady.

"You've been waiting for **ME**?" I say, pointing to myself.

"Yes, we've been waiting for the band to start."

"Is there a band?"

(Get clue here.)

"Are you with the band?

(Miss clue there.)

"No, I'm a guest."

Apparently, I was late.

And I don't even look like Thornetta Davis.

Black People Knit

I said I was a knitter, but that's not what she heard.

We were at a loud party at my friend's house in West Village and I was the only One.

It didn't matter that we were having a polite and interesting conversation, one of those getting-to-know-you, how-do-you-know-so-and-so (read: Why are YOU here?) conversations, where my announcement would have been inappropriate, moreover, *inappropriate*, moreover, awkward, off-topic, out of context, strange.

Arresting.

"I'm a nigger."

What dumb-ass nigger says that at a white-people's party?

No HNIC knitter. No hood-rat knitter. No church-folk knitter. Weed-smokin' knitter. Educated knitter. Politically correct knitter. Hip-hop knitter. White-people-loving knitter. Avant-garde knitter. President of the United

Fucking States knitter.

I knew she thought I said that other word because she didn't react. Usually, when I *announce* myself as a "knitter," people say something.

"I'm a knitter, too."

"My grandmother knits."

"I learned to knit when I was a kid."

"My aunt knits my kids sweaters."

"We have a stitch-and-bitch."

"What do you knit?"

"Do you knit hats?"

"Can you knit me a scarf?"

"How long have you been knitting?"

"Where do you buy your yarn?"

"What are you working on?"

"How many projects you got goin'?"

"Do you knit on straight needles or circulars?"

They say *something*.

She said nothing.

It was her blank pale face that gave me pause. I was a few sentences in before I came to. No questions forthcoming, I looked at her askance.

"Wait: Did you just think I said I was a nigger?"

"Yes."

Ladies and gentlemen, tonight's Golden Globe for **BEST PORTRAYAL OF A POLITICALLY CORRECT WHITE WOMAN IN AN UNCOMFORTABLE SITUATION** goes to the horrified little suburbanite at a house party in Detroit.

I placed my hand on her shoulder, amazed by her composure.

"Girl, you are good! That was so polite."

"I said, 'knitter,'" I said, and started air-knitting.

We laughed and laughed and laughed.

It's not funny.

Fecal Matter

Case. Point.

"Why do you black people always get so offended by shit?"

Cute White Guy from Berkley, in front seat of taxicab, headed home after St. Patrick's Day parade in downtown Detroit, 18 minutes into cab ride.

"Because y'all always say stupid shit."

Oneita Cab Driver, on I-75 north, just past the Clay/Grand Blvd. exit.

Stupid. Shit.

"How do you know about Amici's Pizza?"

Cute White Guy from Berkley, in front seat, headed home after St. Patrick's Day parade in downtown Detroit, 2 minutes into cab ride. Picked up on the corner of Michigan & Trumbull, he asks first to go to the Atheneum Hotel to get his belongings, then, "Can you drive me to Berkley?" Oneita Cab Driver responds: "You mean 'Berkley,' like Amici's Pizza?"

Getting to Know You

"What do you do when you're not at work?"

Oneita Cab Driver, 13 minutes into cab ride, after talking with the Cute White Guy about the parade, which draws hundreds of thousands of people.

Education

"Have you ever heard of Brother Rice?"

Cute White Guy from Berkley, in front seat of taxicab, headed home after St. Patrick's Day parade in downtown Detroit. He tells Oneita Cab Driver he is a coach at the all-boys Catholic high school.

"My son went to U of D Jesuit."

Oneita Cab Driver, 14 minutes into cab ride.

Lowest Common Denomination

"How did you pay for that?"

Cute White Guy from Berkley, in front seat of

taxicab, headed home after St. Patrick's Day parade in downtown Detroit, 15 minutes into cab ride, upon learning Oneita Cab Driver's son attended an all-boys Catholic high school on the west side of Detroit.

High. School.

"I wrote a check."

Oneita Cab Driver, 16 minutes into cab ride.

Class

"Tell me why you're asking me how I paid for my son's education."

Oneita Cab Driver, 17 minutes into cab ride. She has had enough of this shit.

How Did You Pay for That?

robbed bank

danced nights

sold crack

sold loosies

sold stamps

sought sugardaddies

(worked hard)

(worked not)

sold dinners

stole hundreds

stole thousands

started church

impersonated pastor

drove cab

edited copy

wrote columns

called mom

begged uncle

worked nights

worked weekends

facilitated deals

snitched once

snitched twice

offered child

arranged meetings

sang jazz

wrote rhymes

spit verses

borrowed heavily

waited tables

blackmailed media

sponsored terrorism

severed ties

DIRECT DEPOSIT

solved problems

petitioned kim jong un

started nonprofit

swindled nonprofit

surveyed land

engineered deals

created partnerships

facilitated meetings

organized workshops

wooed gilbert

courted quicken

exploited opportunity

placed bets

sold heroin

cheated IRS

smuggled diamonds

rustled cattle

peddled m & m's

wrote books

ordered deaths

sought grants

knit scarves

sold shirts

sacrificed everything

sacrificed nothing

sold weed

sold out

sold lies

sold dreams

printed cash

yen

pesos

renminbi

euros

amex

visa

master charge

diner's club

money orders

used EBT

who said I paid, anyway?

can a nigger get a scholarship?

ADVISORY

Drunk white people scare me.

Drunk white people in downtown Detroit on
Opening Day and St. Patrick's Day scare me.

Drunk white people in the back of my ride scare
me.

But a drunk white woman in the back of my cab
calling me outta my name

at three o'clock in the morning

is not scary.

It's disrespectful.

You keep calling me "Baby Doll" while I keep
telling you "I'm Oneita."

I'm a little sensitive, Miss Daisy.

Oneita Big Dummy

I got pulled over in Grosse Pointe.

Everyone in Detroit knows you do not speed through Grosse Pointe.

You can do 55 on Jefferson, but you better slow your roll when you cross Alter Road.

Grosse Pointers—from all five Pointes—do not speed in Grosse Pointe.

Grosse Pointe police officers do not speed in Grosse Pointe.

No one speeds in Grosse Pointe.

I was speeding in Grosse Pointe.

ROOOORP. ROOOORP.

LIGHTS! CAMERA! ACTION!
(And I'm singing I'm sorry, Miss Jackson.)

The officer is at my window.

My arms are stretched straight out, my E.T.-

phone-home hands spread wide.

"Why are you holding your hands up?"

I am a dark-brown woman in a beyond-lily-white upper-class suburb of Detroit, where just a couple years ago, a few police officers forced black men to sing and dance and make strange noises, and this white man is asking me why I am dramatically demonstrating to him that I am not a threat.

It was a natural reflex and I do not understand the question.

Reflections

When I look in my mirror

In the morning,

I see Oneita.

When I look in my rearview mirror

later, I see red, white, and blue lights

and I see a police officer.

Flashing.
Lights.

HANDS ON THE WHEEL.
DON'T MOVE AN INCH.

When the police officer

looks at me,

he sees a scofflaw:

40

in

a

25.

Flashing.
Lights.

DO NOT TOUCH THE WINDOW.
DO NOT GRAB YOUR PURSE.

OFFICER APPROACHING. SIT STILL.

"Why are you holding your hands up?"

the privilege of obliviousness

I'm real confused, I

always speak truth, I

don't want to die, I

today I lie, I

Uhhh …

…

…

…

Ummm …

"There's nothing there, officer."

I am a Generation X black woman in Grosse Pointe.

He is an X+ white police officer.

With a gun.

This is the United States of America.

"Yes, sir."

"Yes, sir."

"Yes, sir."

25

in

a

25.

Oneita Big Happy:

He lets me go!

Oneita Jackson is a satirist and Detroit cab driver who has an English degree from Howard University. She was a copy editor for 11 years at the Detroit Free Press. During that time, she served as public editor, wrote music reviews, edited on the Features, Nation/World, and Web desks, received awards for her headlines, and was a member of the Accuracy and Credibility Committee. She also wrote the "O Street" column for three years; it received the newspaper's 2008 Columnist of the Year award. She stopped writing the column in May 2010 and returned to the News Copy Desk, where she stayed until August 2012. Her next adventure was driving a yellow cab. The *Nappy-Headed Negro Syndrome* satires are observations and commentary on people and culture. These stories about identity are written by a woman who is uniquely, unabashedly, and extraordinarily herself.

A native of Dayton, Ohio, Oneita spent her summers in New York City and has lived in Washington, D.C., and Albany, N.Y. She now lives in Detroit.

"People think I drive a cab,
but I actually work in my head."

Oneita Jackson, driving back from Detroit
Metro Airport a few months after leaving her
newspaper job, in 2012.

9 780578 166575